There Was a Baby...

Written and Illustrated by Laura Camerona, CCLS

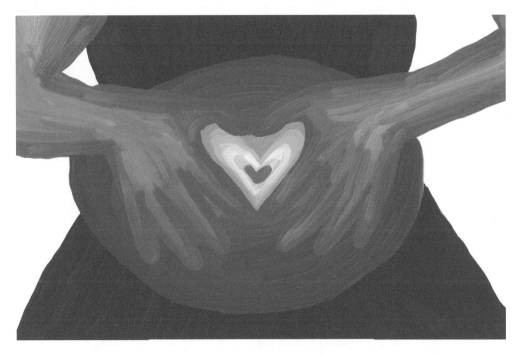

A
**Words Worth
Repeating**
Book

www.wordsworthrepeating.com

Tips for Reading this Book and Having Other Important Conversations with a Child:

- Follow the child's lead. If they aren't in the mood to read the book, save it for another moment.
- Stop and answer questions. If in the middle of the book your child wants to talk about one part of the book or one question that they have, set the book aside and focus on that.
- Bedtime often isn't the best time for books about topics that kids may have questions about. It might lead to trouble sleeping. The first time you read this book with your child, try to avoid right before bedtime.
- Have your child choose a person or people that they can talk to when they have questions or want to talk about their feelings. They may choose their parent, but sometimes, children want to protect their family from being sad and would rather choose a good friend or family memeber who is less affected.
-Don't expect a certain outword reaction from your child. It is okay if your child doesn't show the emotions that you might expect.
-We are here for you. If your child asks questions or reacts in a way that you don't feel comfortable with, reach out to us at www.wordsworthrepeating.com or contact a local mental health professional.

Dedicated to my sweet baby who impacted the world without being out in it.

There was a baby inside
of Momma's tummy.

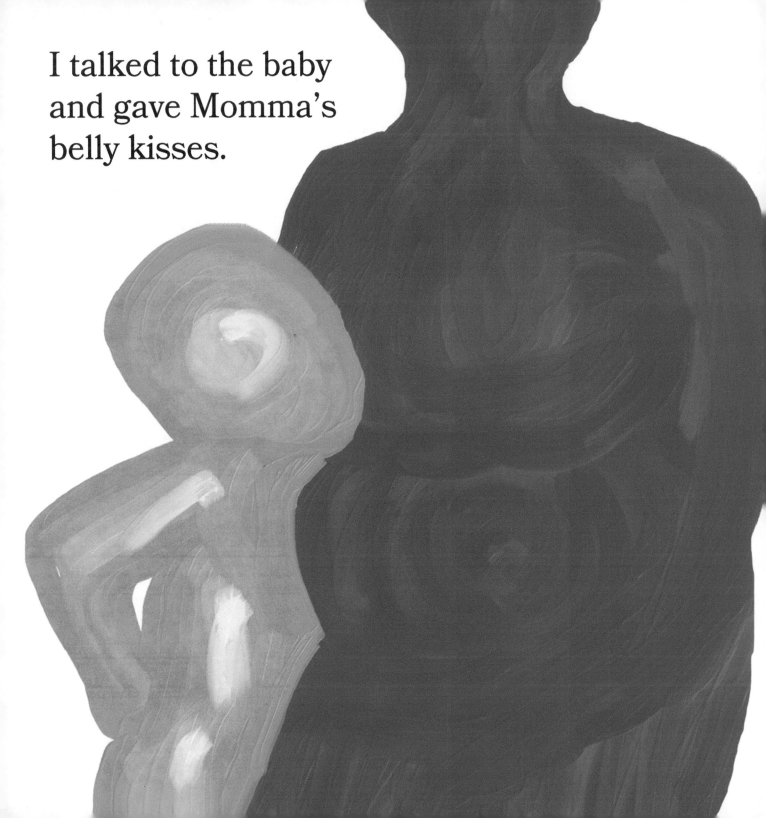

I talked to the baby
and gave Momma's
belly kisses.

The baby
was warm
and cozy
inside.

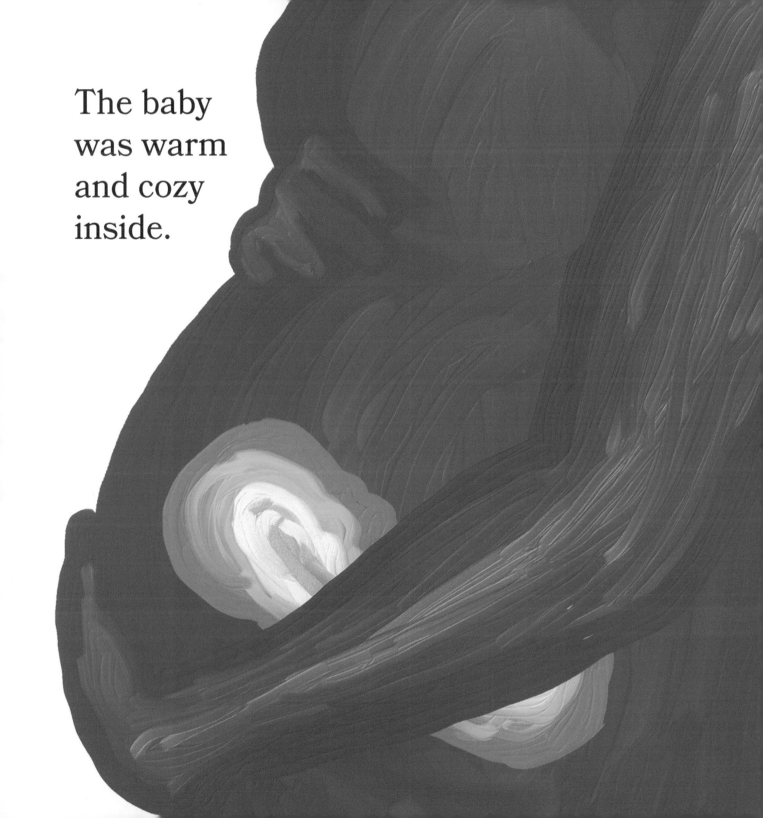

Lots babies grow in tummies and come out when they are big and healthy.

Our baby didn't grow this way.

We don't know why. It's no one's fault. Sometimes, sad things happen.

My family is sad. They wish that our baby could be alive and healthy and would come home to live with us.

Some days when my family feels sad, I feel sad too. Some days when my family is sad, I feel happy. It's okay to feel how I feel.

We aren't the only family that this has happened to. When babies grow inside tummies, this happens sometimes.

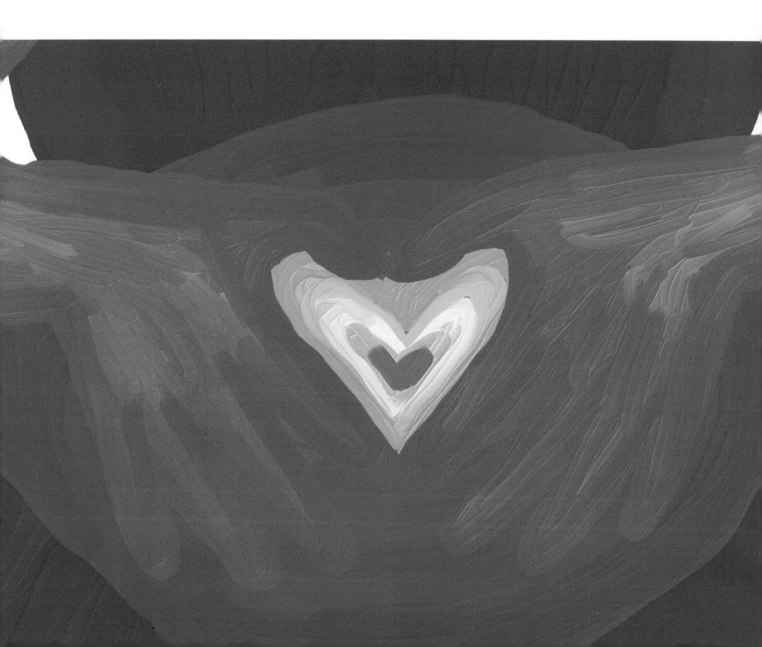

If there is a baby in your momma's tummy, it makes you a big brother or a big sister. Even though our baby died, that doesn't change.

We are still big brothers and big sisters.

Our baby is still special and important.

Our baby reminds my family how strong our love is.

Our
baby
felt
our
love.

Sometimes,
I think about
our baby. I
think about
what it
would have
been like if
the baby
would have
grown big
and healthy.

My family still thinks about our baby, too. In that way, our baby is with us forever. We will all have memories of our baby who lived in Momma's tummy.

We can come up with ways to remember our baby. Our family can talk about our baby, we could make a special piece of artwork, or we could light a candle.

Our baby will always be a part of our family.

Special Projects Families Can Create Together

Some families have the opportunity to get their baby's hand prints or foot prints. Even if you have only one set of actual prints, you can use scanner or an app on your phone to make more copies. Here are some examples of things you can create with these prints.

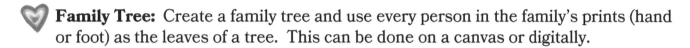 **Family Tree:** Create a family tree and use every person in the family's prints (hand or foot) as the leaves of a tree. This can be done on a canvas or digitally.

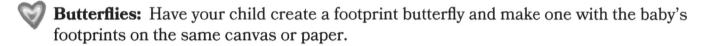 **Butterflies:** Have your child create a footprint butterfly and make one with the baby's footprints on the same canvas or paper.

 Frame Art: Buy or repurpose a frame with wide and flat sides. Have your child decorate the frame however they wish. Display the baby's prints in this frame.

Some families like to create a special place in their home or yard to remember their baby. Children can help create artwork that is displayed in this area. Here are some art projects that they can create.

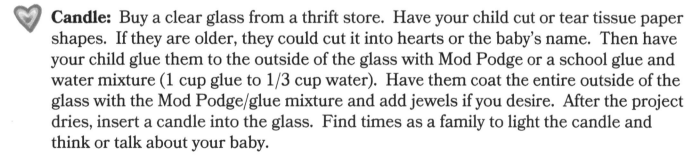 **Candle:** Buy a clear glass from a thrift store. Have your child cut or tear tissue paper shapes. If they are older, they could cut it into hearts or the baby's name. Then have your child glue them to the outside of the glass with Mod Podge or a school glue and water mixture (1 cup glue to 1/3 cup water). Have them coat the entire outside of the glass with the Mod Podge/glue mixture and add jewels if you desire. After the project dries, insert a candle into the glass. Find times as a family to light the candle and think or talk about your baby.

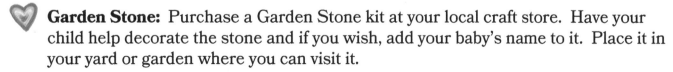 **Garden Stone:** Purchase a Garden Stone kit at your local craft store. Have your child help decorate the stone and if you wish, add your baby's name to it. Place it in your yard or garden where you can visit it.

 Tree/Flower: As a family, plant a flower or tree in memory of your baby.

Special Projects Families Can Create Together (continued)

Some families like to create something that they can wear or keep close on days when they want to feel close to their baby. Here are some ideas of things of things that children can help make.

 Family Necklace/Bracelet: Provide your child a variety of beads (most craft stores have a "mix pack") and a string. Have your child choose a bead for each family member. The bead could be symbolic based on color, shape, anything! If they don't do it on their own, ask if they would like to include a bead for the baby. If they chose not to, that is okay. You can talk about what a great team your family is during this

 Paper Beads: Better activity for older children. Provide scrapbook paper. Have the child chose paper that is special to them. Have them cut a long thin triange (approximately 3/4 in wide and 9 in long). On the white side, have them write a message to themselves, the baby's name, anything! Starting on the wide end wind the paper tightly, so that the message on the inside of the bead and the colorful side

Some families like to create something that they won't see every day, but that they will see every so often or on special holidays to remember their baby. Here are some ideas of things that kids can help create.

 Holiday Ornament: Find a simple flat ornament or a ball and add the baby's name to it. Allow your child to decorate.

 Blank Book/ScrapBook: Use a blank book or journal and fill the pages with family memories of being pregnant, photos, pictures your child draws, write out feelings everyone is feeling, anything. Get the book out on days when your family wants to spend more time remembering your baby.

Laura Camerona,
Certified Child
Life Specialist

After 15 years working in a hospital and helping children and families through a variety of experiences, Laura started creating books to help families and promote healing, as they continue their journey outside of the hospital.

Laura is now especially focused on helping families have hard conversations and get through challenging times together. As a Mom of three, she promotes giving kids honest, gentle, and developmentally appropriate explanations. She believes in family resiliency and believes that families develop the best coping when they go through things together. To learn more about Laura's other resources and services, check out the next page!

Words Worth Repeating creates books to promote positive coping and healing for kids and families.

Families work with a Child Life Specialist to create customized books that give families good words in hard situations.

Words Worth Repeating specializes in Legacy Books (books about a loved one who has died) and Journey Books (books about something the child or a loved one is experiencing).

Contact us to learn more!

Words Worth Repeating

www.wordsworthrepeating.com